L Letterally

Joan Colby

FUTURECYCLE PRESS

www.futurecycle.org

Cover and interior book design by Diane Kistner

Stempel Garamond text with Futura numbering, Kingthings Pique'n'meex capitals

Library of Congress Control Number: 2020949775

Published by FutureCycle Press
Athens, Georgia, USA

ISBN 978-1-952593-14-7

Saint Augustine addressed his savior:
Make me ascetic, Lord, but not yet.

The ailing once took refuge in
Alpine hospices to inhale the pure air.

Athena is the goddess of wisdom.
Her avatar is the owl.

Those who advertise their virtues
May live to feast on the apples of regret.

The apples of the Hesperides were golden
To weigh down the brazen adventurers.

Australia bore the stain of the aborted.
Anglo Saxons and Celts convicted of crimes.

The aborigines became the next victims.
An abused child learns the lesson well.

Anne Boleyn failed to produce a male heir
That could outlive the ailments of infancy.

Poor Anne was sentenced to the axe.
Charged with multiple adulteries.

Thus autocrats have always dispensed
With those who confronted their arrogance.

Annihilation is the fate of all
Who exist: an arbitrary law.

Imagine if bluebirds became the legislators
Of Baltimore and Burning Man the habitation of

Birds of prey, falcons swooping from the clouds.
The Blue Man troop will celebrate its Druidic

Origin waving the blue leaves of the World Tree.
Saint Thomas à Becket, Saint Bernadette,

Benjamin the favorite son sail above the bluffs
Along the Mississippi in the beautiful Driftless Area.

Up on the rimrocks, we board the plane heading east
As bell ringers dance on ropes

In the blessed chapel marking time.
A brigade of angels brandishes

Weapons of justice. Bees hold the world in their wings.
A bread basket of honey.

And now you run with the bulls of Pamplona
As bishops lead the procession of the

Blue Madonna. A woman in a burka gathers grapes, bananas.
Oh listen, you must rescue the baby from the

Ruined building where unexploded bombs
Endanger the beseechers.

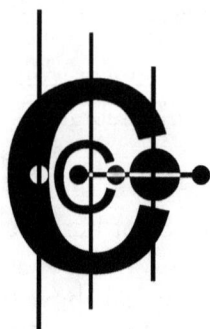

Cecilia, saint of the harpsichord
And clarinet. The chimes of the Angelus.

Bring me camellias, rich and creamy
As clouds reflected in still waters.

Cautionary tales instruct the courageous
To understand that fearlessness is the crypt of imagination.

Children call like a flock of sparrows
Contesting in an autumn pile of catalpa leaves.

The shy cardinal comes at dusk to the feeder.
Crimson feathers, crested cap.

Corrosive words invigorate the quarrel
Of old companions, cynical with age.

The limestone church erected by Czech immigrants
Elevates Christ in the crystal chapel of the poor.

Spitting cobras sway in a circus
Of confrontation. Come away.

A congregation of coral reefs
Invite the colorful.

Change the calendar and the climate hangs,
Victimized by corporations.

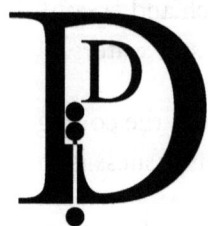

The deviant invent the dream of art,
A dicey chance of perpetual display.

The Lion Hunt by Delacroix
Defines the baroque with defiance.

A dapper man: bespoken suit
And old-school tie, deeply polished shoes.

Destiny brings a host of denials.
Do or die chant the disenfranchised.

The disinherited dig the bitter earth
To locate the dirt of disappointment.

Diamonds glitter on engaged fingers
Or on the tips of raucous drills.

Doubt is the grievance of devotion.
Turn the pages of the daily breviary.

A doe crosses the road at dawn,
Light falling on her flanks like silver dollars.

Early days of evolution
Introduced the eel. Slunk

In its mud cave, that shocking grin
Reptilian, antediluvian.

Eight women carrying baskets of lilies
Ennoble the cathedrals of Europe

While evening gathers the nightjars
To sing sad eulogies.

Esther, symbol of loyalty, stares
Over the centuries where eagles feed

And hummingbirds hang in envelopes of air.
Exactitude is the virtue

Of eminence. Enter the house
Of the pure. Here we will eat

Bread spread with honey. We will
Engage in the conversation

Of the enlightened. It is easy
To recite what we have learned

As we are educated in subversion,
Exiled in a prison of false persuasion.

Consider the elephant descendant of the
Mastodon, the earnest man

Descendant of the angels.

Ff

Follow the road to foreclosure.
See how the fallow deer graze

In the fairy circles where children hunt painted eggs.
Grace and favor bestowed by royalty

Was the fiction we believed,
A symbol of goodness and faith.

Friendship endures fire and famine.
In the face of contradiction, we find our

Hands grasping flowers.
Sit down to French toast and fried bacon.

This is the breakfast of the fortunate.
Life is finite. We must embrace it fully

Or find ourselves forlorn
On the fever coast.

The policy of a ghost is to walk lightly
So only the most sensitive will despair

Of the indignities of generation—how the body passes
From gross to guile. The Green Man haunts

The lonely garden. Interpret his garbled language
If you dare. What is genuine can be guarded

With intelligence, a genius for discovery.
Gold destroys the forests of Brazil. Grasslands

Abbreviate the glory of the canopy.
Goodness is scraped from topsoil.

The ghost that whispers to gentle souls
Glows like a will-o'-the-wisp, then goes out

Like a candle in a storm.
Get me another, shouts the gremlin

Of our old wishes, our old granite
Improvisations, our old beliefs in the gaudy

Gloves of the gods.

The harlequin Dane's heavy head
Lies between its paws. *Hey,*

Says his master. It's a hot day
In Hennepin County. Heaven isn't

Just a myth to those who handle
Snakes. Hang around here awhile and

Hold the hand of evil. You will be
Harbored. Today, the men are haying.

The women hug each other. Holy
Jesus loves the helpless. Honey

In the mouths of children. Happiness
Is not a habit when the hope of

Salvation is hung from the rafters of the
Hexagonal barn. A white heifer

Is sacrificed with a harpoon of
Hallelujahs.

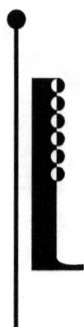

Incantations chime through the island
Of good ideas. Iceland leads the world

In literacy. On Christmas Eve a new book
Is received and everyone insists

On going to bed and reading. Images are important
To the illiterate. Illness befalls the innocent.

The petition is written in India ink. It implores
Us to immerse ourselves in new identities.

Look inward, angels. Build igloos of ice
For the ignorant. Imprint us with the

Incense of joy. It is not indelible,
That iguana in your dream.

Jj

Justice is served, claims Janus,
His two faces joined at the junction

Of faith and denial. This is the jubilee
That Justinian prophesied. Little John

Followed the precepts of Jesus. The trials
Of Job afflict the judicious.

Judy Garland jumped the time warp
To Oz and jackrabbits are the curse

Of the outback. At the River Jordan
A jury meets to judge the unlawful.

Jupiter, the greatest planet, journeys through space
Like Joan of Arc praising the voices of her saints.

Kk

Knock on the black door to release the kites
Who scour the sky for the dying. A keen

Vision to administer the lethal kiss.
An old woman knits the weather

Into a scarf of clouds. The kiln of storms.
She knows the history of kangaroos,

The marsupial text where keepers
Of the lost kingdom

Illuminate the manuscripts. Collect the
Knickknacks of the first religion:

The tree of knowledge where the King
Cobra dispenses wisdom and trickery.

The hiss that kills.

Love is the seminal word. Its lone
Syllable on the legendary march

To locate the lyric that makes it whole.
Live under its umbrella. You will learn

To scrub the laundry clean of fear,
To delouse the night terrors that litter

The dreams of children. Look for the slash marks
On the Lindens — they light the path

You will follow. Listen and the language
Will be so pure, so literal, you can't help

But lounge in its diction, take a lover.

He worked on the miniatures for a movie star's
Dollhouse. It's in the Museum of Science

And Industry. His artistry involved the musculature
Of magical fingers. Each motif perfect with its mimicry.

This obsession with mowing down size locks the mind
On a censure of the mini-edition of *Moby Dick*

That mirrors each page of the master.
Those who sacrifice the mission of comfort to maintain

A mini-house must be magnanimous in devotion
To the miniscule. Maybe it's just a maneuver

To be earth mother of novelty. Maybe it's a miscue,
Like disputed gender. A motley crew of midgets

Madhouse with Dorothy. Those merry little men,
What a move they'd like to make.

No. *Nada. Nein.* Never.
Words nobody wants to hear.

A negative view where all skies darken.
A neighborhood of rain.

North windows of cold light.
Nothing of charm or pleasure.

A neutered afternoon of
Normal boredom. No one smiles.

The theme is *No Exit*—like a
Needle in a haystack

Or a needle in the eye.
A new world order.

Nothing equals nothing.

It could be a letter or a zero or the gasp
Of a person surprised or a person alarmed.

The omens of sorrow. O—so ordinary.
The shape of the circle unending.

Obvious, certainly, but never ornate.
Over not under. Out not in.

One of the Great Lakes: Ontario.
Orion, the hunter of the skies.

My father's name: Otho after an
Insignificant Roman emperor.

Osprey, an endangered bird.
The orioles who return each year

For orange slices and marmalade.
October, month of outrageous

Color. The overstory of the aspens.
The old gold of the burr oaks.

Open the door and *oh!*
It's better than expected

Like the overture of the opera
Where you always attend the opening

In order to be seen.

Period. Stops the sentence with a shriek of brakes.
Levered to end an argument over politics

Or anything. Period saves the adolescent girl
Who weeps texting the most probable boy.

Perfection must not be the enemy of the good
Goes the platitude. Settle for the passable

Is the prurient message. Pink is the hue that leaks
When the savagery of red has been penetrated.

Pursue basics. Pursue pungency. Defy the pink
Of the undercooked. Pemphigus afflicts the

Mucous membranes. Rare as readers of *The Faerie Queene.*
Perhaps or possibly qualify intentions, halter

Passion. Oh proceed like Picasso from phase to
Phase. Life's purpose is discovery.

A quarry man—that ancestor
Who left the quaint starvation of Mayo

For a coffin boat to Queens
Where the Union Army quartermaster

Seized him to march through the quilted
Cotton fields to Georgia. After the treaties were signed,

He quit to go north where no quarrelsome landlords
Presided over peat bogs. He found a quiet woman

Who never quailed when her infants perished.
As a child I thought this a queer story—these people

Who queued up for sorrow and turned it into quips.
Surely, I was of their quality: one who would rather be

A quiz kid than the bloody Queen of England.

I ride my horse up on the rims
Along the fenced-off runways

Where a DC-10 releases travelers to the tarmac.
At night on the ridge, you can see

The light-ribboned city radiating far below.
A boy raves he'll jump

Unless his girl gives in. Next day, he rats out
The conquest to his buddies. She is ravished,

Her reputation in rags. This was the Fifties.
Senior year, a reckless car, racing,

Roars off a switchback to a rodeo of flame.
We rendezvous at the Big Boy burger stand,

Rating our memories against each other.
Live fast, die young, we say, our repertoire

Of cool. We ring-a-rosy Broadway in our
Rattletraps, honking and waving.

We are rich in our youth, in our lack of regret,
The rimrocks facing north where the remorseless winds

Blow down from the Arctic,
Rousting us off into the rigors of real life.

Sundays are sedentary.
Church services or the symphony

On shady afternoons. Sweet tea
Beneath the sycamores with someone singing

Softly in the background. Slow dancing.
How water spills from a fountain or a spring.

Swallows at dusk and sunsets.
The sea on a still day, its small waves lapping

At the shoreline. Shells and words spoken
Sincerely. Love in the shadows. Sequels

That outshine the original. Beautiful shoes.

Tough love. Tree trimmers risking their lives
With chainsaws in the treetops. Taking chances

On unsure things. Tickets to nowhere. A tale
Of twenty cities where you traveled. Thin air

At the treeline where the tiny mountain flowers
Thrive in crevices. The toad songs of spring

Peepers. Tight spots. Trapped in burning tenements.
Try anything. Tap dancing while children

Throw a ball through a hoop. Two lovers
Winning teddy bears at a carnival. Riding

The Tilt-A-Whirl, eating taffy apples, touring
The midway. Tears for no reason. Trust me.

The universe in a scratchy union suit.
Uncounted stars. The planet Uranus.

A boy rides a unicycle down the
Unpainted boardwalk. Extreme Unction,

The final sacrament. A ukulele
Of good time music. Undone buttons.

Units of energy. Urban warriors.
Uncertifiable documents. Join the Union,

Brother, sister. Unite. Uncover the heart's
Unique passion. Under the world tree

Of the Ukraine, Kalyna, you find
Unbelievable treasures. Use your talents.

The Viceroy imitates the Monarch
In a version of survival.

A vision of the Madonna
Veils the children with virtue.

What are your values, citizens?
Venice sinks beneath the waves.

Volcanoes erupt on Caribbean
Islands. Girls are violated.

They run away. Virginia
Scarred forever. Her stories vindicated

The trapped women. Venture out
Of your village. Undo the violence

Of your concealed hair. Your room
With a view. Victory is found

At the gateway of the vagina.

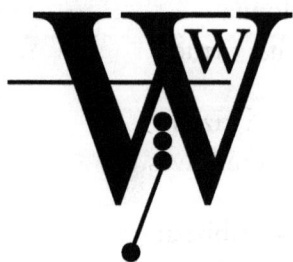

Wait up, we said as children
Wanting inclusion, the generous words

We barely understood. We wished
For everything. The diamond waters

Sparkling offshore where whales
Spouted and warships cruised

The horizon. A great wave rises
In the Japanese woodcut. A warning

To the wise, perhaps, or a willingness
To imagine. Don't waver. We need to

Worship, to will ourselves westward
Where the sun falls off the edge

Of the world. *Wait up,* we whisper.

There's an external way of escaping
The bars of existence.

Exit through the cumulus clouds
That extinguish the bare lightbulb of cynics

Hanging over an expected meal,
Overcooked and expensive.

An ox team awaits you, survivor,
If you rid yourself of excess:

The extemporaneous views
Of the literati with axes to grind.

Board the wagon ready to explore
The western boundaries of the unisex mind.

Leave the toxic cities where you wasted
The excellence of your heritage.

When you write, sign off with XXXes.

Youth is wasted on the young—
So goes the adage. A yellow tinge

On the eyeball. A yellowish fog
Envelopes the year of scorpions.

Say yes to the war on whatever.
You know you're headed somewhere:

Yellowstone or Yuma.
The westward expansion

Where a singing cowboy yodels.
No one ever yearned for this, did they?

Not the yuppies next door
With their little Yorkie, a yellow bow

In its topknot. Transplanted Yankees.
At our yearly barbecue, she says

Oh Yummy and he yells at our cat.
They get drunk and sing "YMCA"

With gestures.

The zone of iniquity,
A place composed of zeros

Where the Zen koan is divined
To try the zeal of the righteous.

The Zika virus denies a child
A life of joyous zest.

One flying insect in a zoo of predators
Outweighs the theory of zymotic disease.

As the zip-tied words confine the reader
Of Zola to the 19th century. *J'accuse.*

Enter the circuit of the Zodiac
To find your avatar, the zany archer,

Or justice in the canton of Zürich.
Feast on zwieback spread with hummus,

A zombie breakfast.
In Zimbabwe, you'll ride

A zebra sidesaddle. You'll journey to the
Land of Zion. Oh hero, you will reach

The zenith of ambition,
Fall headlong for Zenobia,

Queen of Palmyra. Dream on, zealot
It's a perfect day for zebrafish.

About FutureCycle Press

FutureCycle Press is dedicated to publishing lasting English-language poetry in both print-on-demand and Kindle formats. Founded in 2007 by long-time independent editor/publishers and partners Diane Kistner and Robert S. King, the press incorporated as a nonprofit in 2012. A number of our editors are distinguished poets and writers in their own right, and we have been actively involved in the small press movement going back to the early seventies.

We award the FutureCycle Poetry Book Prize and honorarium annually for the best full-length volume of poetry we published that year. Introduced in 2013, proceeds from our Good Works projects are donated to charity. Our Selected Poems series highlights contemporary poets with a substantial body of work to their credit; with this series we strive to resurrect work that has had limited distribution and is now out of print.

We are dedicated to giving all of the authors we publish the care their work deserves, offering a catalog of the most diverse and distinguished work possible, and paying forward any earnings to fund more great books. All of our books are kept "alive" and available unless and until an author requests a title be taken out of print.

We've learned a few things about independent publishing over the years. We've also evolved a unique and resilient publishing model that allows us to focus mainly on vetting and preserving for posterity poetry collections of exceptional quality without becoming overwhelmed with bookkeeping and mailing, fundraising activities, or taxing editorial and production "bubbles." To find out more about what we are doing, come see us at www.futurecycle.org.

The FutureCycle Poetry Book Prize

All full-length volumes of poetry published by FutureCycle Press in a given calendar year are considered for the annual FutureCycle Poetry Book Prize. This allows us to consider each submission on its own merits, outside of the context of a traditional contest. Too, the judges see the finished book, which will have benefitted from the beautiful book design and strong editorial gloss we are famous for.

The book ranked the best in judging is announced as the prize-winner in the subsequent year. There is no fixed monetary award; instead, the winning poet receives an honorarium of 20% of the total net royalties from all poetry books and chapbooks the press sold online in the year the winning book was published. The winner is also accorded the honor of being on the panel of judges for the next year's competition; all judges receive copies of all contending books to keep for their personal library.